# Being Out
## of
# THE BOX

## SANDRA MARIE HOLLOWAY

Print information available on the last page

Rev. date: 08/01/2018/

To order additional copies of this book, contact:
Xlibris
1-888-795-4274
www.Xlibris.com
Orders@Xlibris.com

SANDRA MARIE
SPIRITUALIST READER / ADVISOR
MEDIUM / SENSITIVE
CLAIRVOYANT / CHANNELING
MULTIDIMENSIONAL READER
SPIRITUAL ACCESSIONS EXPERIENCE
ENLIGHTENMENT GROWTH
BEING OUT OF THE BOX

# Dedicated To:

Father / Mother God and Jesus.
Yahweh - God - uncreated One.
Yashua – Son of God.
Elsworth my mentor.
All Holy Entities of Love & Light.
I am honored and so proud of my two children
and my three wonderful grandchildren.

SANDRA MARIE 2018

I wrote a document about myself so that I can share with others that are or have been in similar situations as I have been in the past. To witness to anyone who will listen that we all encounter different situations during our life time here on this Planet Earth.

Each individual situation allows us to grow and learn true Spiritual knowledge and Wisdom.

Actions are Choices - Cause and Effect of Divine Wisdom.

This document will be like I am talking to you directly!! Simple conversation between you and me!!

Love & Light - Sandy Marie - sandrahollowaygrizzle@yahoo.com

SANDRA MARIE AURA PICTURE

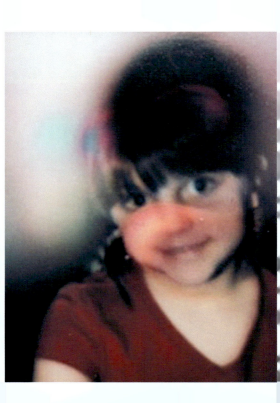

SANDRA MARIE

URA COLORS SHOW THE ELECTRICAL ENERGY OF OU

ATING VIBRATIONS THAT CHANGE MOMENT BY MON

EACH INDIVIDUAL SITUATION ALLOWS US TO GROW AND LEARN TRUE SPIRITUAL KNOWLEDGE AND WISDOM.

ACTIONS ARE CHOICES

CAUSE AND EFFECT OF DIVINE WISDOM

This text will be like I am talking to you directly.

No Book Form – Just a simple conversation between you and me!!

To begin with I am a normal hard-working person, I raised two great children, and have three grandchildren. I finally have made peace with my past, forgiven myself, and many others. I look forward to the present, and future.

I have left out some details because most human beings will not accept or listen to unconventional statements.

Here WE Go:

I was born on September 27, 1948 my first memory is when I was four years old.

I remember being tied to a towel rack attached to the back of a door, white towels were tied around me making it impossible for me to move. My mouth was covered with a wide towel. I had no pants on I did have a shirt on. It was dark, the blinds were all pulled down, you could see in the room, but no lights were on.

Arizona with my daughter and granddaughter.

My cousin who was at least sixteen and playing with his front area of his body. I was scared, I remember having trouble breathing. I heard my daddy calling my name. My cousin kept whispering be quiet to me, and be still to me. I couldn't make any noise anyway or move. I heard daddy walking off, I was so scared he would be mad at me.

After a while, my cousin untied me, made me promise I would not tell my daddy we were in that room, and not to tell anyone what we were doing. Then my cousin made me lay down on the floor. Finally, he let me go.

As soon as he let me go, I went home my daddy was laying down on his bed reading the newspaper. He asked me where I had been, I told him. Then I told him I feared my cousin, and what he did to me with the towels, and the floor. I told him I wanted to answer, but I could not, and that my cousin made me be quiet. Daddy told me to never go anywhere with my cousin again. To always stay with the grownups.

My grandfather died in this home he was 58, my daddy died when he was 58, he was born in this home. Daddy's half-brother died when he was 58. The home still stands.

I did go back to the home place and both my grandfather and uncle left the dwelling in spirit upon my request in Jesus name.

When I was eighteen I was staying in the home on the other side. Not the same room.

Some other persons were renting it. You could always hear someone walking in that part of the house when no one was there. I and three other persons stood at the doors and entered from each door to see if someone was in the rooms. There was no way for anyone there not to be seen. Each time no one was seen. The walking could still be heard with the doors locked since 70's.

This had been my grandmother's home for many years until it was sold. I visited the house and the room where this situation happened. The room looked so small to me, and it still looked the same isn't that unreal. By visiting the room, it helped to heal me.

We moved to a real nice house in the country. My parents had their own room and so did I. Between our ages of six to eight we lived there, and it was nice. I made a long tent in the back yard. It was made of up branches, tarps, and plastics to set on. Played a lot in the tents made, when the weather tore them down, I would make another.

While playing felt safe in the tent with no one else around. I always took the blame mainly because I was the oldest.

At eight years old I started feeling what I called people around me. I couldn't see them, but I could sense whether they were male, female, or children. I would feel someone watching me especially at home outside my bedroom window. One day I was outside, I always watched the sky, looking for something I didn't know what, I just felt I wasn't supposed to be here, that I belonged somewhere else. It always seemed I was waiting to see something. One day I saw a cigar shaped vehicle in the sky, it was real close to the ground, it was headed straight over our house. First, I thought it was a blimp, a Goodyear vehicle, but it was solid, no windows, no flags, and was silver. It was as low as our roof.

I ran to get my mother, told her something was in the sky coming over our house. She said I be there in a minute.

I went back outside on the front doorsteps there it was headed straight for the roof. It was coming between the tree and the point of the front roof. It ran into the tree limbs, and the side of the roof point. The edge of the roof was bent, and tree limbs fell to the ground. Then it was gone, at that time my mother came out and said where is it, I said it left, she looked all over the sky, it wasn't anywhere to be seen. Then I showed her the roof, and limbs on the ground. That time there was proof. I showed it to my daddy when he got home. Everyone told me not to say anything to anyone.

I used to tell my mother about a lot of things I felt and saw. Especially in the sky, she would tell me not to tell people, others would think something was wrong with me. I could tell her, but not others. Always wanted to be outside in the forest.

I noticed silver objects in the sky a lot. First, I thought they were planes. These objects I saw would keep my attention, for a long time, planes moved away, these objects seemed to want to get my attention.

Around this age I asked my mother to get shades for my room, because I felt like someone was always looking in my window. My mother did, that made me sleep better. I was always afraid to be in my room alone, I always felt others in the room with me, not just one, many. I always put my shades down before dark, one night I was watching television, it had to have been on a Friday night we got to stay up late on that night. I walked back to my bedroom, my shades were still up, and there in my window was something looking at me. I screamed, my mother came running, she got there but it was gone. She pulled my shades down so I could go into my room.

I always closed my windows too, I felt someone would take off the screens and come in.

The person looking at me was different than me, it had no hair, round head, very short, and eyes were big and wide, skin looked like rubber I could see it because of the light outside. After that night until we moved away there was always a shadow outside my windows, you could see the shadows thru the blinds. The shape was different than mine the head came a little bit up over the window base. It was real round, and never moved. One window was on the North side of the house near the field, and the other was on the West looking out the back yard.

During this time there was a lot of motion going on in the field and the back yard. Always real early in the morning before the sun came up. I could feel objects coming back and forth in the field, and a lot of people walking from the objects, and lots loading on the objects. People would walk into the surrounding wooded areas they were the same looking people I saw at my windows. They were short, long arms, no children all adults. It was always real foggy, one object would come down, unload, reload then another one would come down, three at a time, for a short period of time. The ones reloading would be real tired looking, wore out, having a hard time getting up the walkway.

I started asking my mother if I could have a statue of Jesus to protect me when it was dark, she got me a statue of Jesus and I always kept a white candle burning until we moved to the forest. My aunt came over one day and fussed at me saying I was an sinner which scared me to death so I busted the statue, then started praying all the time.

When I was around eight years old I started to get real sick, I always had real bad ear aches, my daddy would come home after work and sit there for a long time rubbing behind my ear to make the pain go away. It was really bad pain, I remember every Saturday I would go to the doctor's lab to get blood test. I was real skinny my mother told me the doctor said I had the first stages of leukemia.

I missed a lot of school I had to stay back in the fourth grade because I missed to many days.

I don't know when I started sleep- walking. My daddy would fine me outside of the house in the front yard. I do remember being awake by the fence where I had been looking North from our yard. That was the vacant land that was always so busy at night.

I would wake up in my parent's room standing beside my daddy from sleepwalking, he always watched for me, so he wouldn't hurt me from his being jumpy from the War.

When I visited my aunt and uncle up north, I sleep walked and scared them.

We moved after a few years to the forest, around thirty miles from our nice home.

We lived in an old wooden house the wind and rain would come in between the boards. It was a hunting camp house. My daddy fixed it up, so the walls were better, put in a commode, and made it livable. Both parents ran a restaurant real close to our house.

I was sleep walking when Hurricane Donna came thru our area. I was only around 10 years old and didn't know what a Hurricane was. Before the hurricane came this is what happened to me.

I was outside in front of our house in the road my daddy woke me up very gently, so he wouldn't scare me. He never touched me to wake me up.

I was seeing a real big funnel, wind noise that sounded like a train. Lightening flashing, people screaming. Daddy kept calling my name real slow several times and I woke up. I was trembling from what I had seen, and I usually remember them all.

I was around nine or ten years old then. We left for school before daylight and got home after dark. There was a family that was always being late for the bus. These children had a grandfather who had a fishing camp the fishing camp had several old buildings that they rented to people for staying there while fishing. These children were always at the fishing camp especially on the week- ends. There were several males, and several females. Like door steps. I loved this family because of their love for each other true Indians of Florida their parents really had a hard time financially. Kids had yellow hair.

My parents needed some help in the restaurant, so they hired this old man in his seventies to work in the restaurant and fix meals for us. This man lived in the back of our house and entered thru the back door. I was around twelve years old. My parents were at work this man told me that he had a present for me, that all I had to do was come lay down beside him, and he would give me my present. He told me not to tell my parents, that he wanted to give me something himself. So, it was time to go to bed, and the old man called me into his room, I stood by his bed, he patted the bed beside him and said come on up here, I said I didn't want to, he started pulling me up on the bed, pushing me down, and kissing me on the mouth.

I fought him, kicked him, and got away. I ran into the bathroom, I was screaming, I just kept washing my mouth out with soap, trying to get clean. I finally stopped crying, I just ran out the front door and started getting on my bike to get to my mother. The old man stood at the back-door screen yelling, "Do not go to your parents."

ran over to the restaurant told my mother what happened, my daddy ran out, I felt so dirty, and ashamed. I couldn't look my daddy, or mother in the face. Daddy went over to the house, was beating the man, and the sheriff got there and pulled the knife out of daddy's hand before he stabbed the old man. I had to sit at the table across from my mother, and daddy, and the old man at the end of the table, and the sheriff besides me and tell them what had happened. I was so ashamed, felt so dirty, I just knew my daddy was going to be real mad and displeased with me, I couldn't look anyone in the face.

The old man had to leave that night the police took him away.

My daddy made me a room out where the old man had a room. My mother put dolls on the wall, daddy had a peg- board I got small dolls from every country I could. My parents had their own room too. I didn't have to sleep on the couch anymore.

I had a friend who asked me to spend a week with her, the parents were real nice, and they vacationed in the area we lived. They lived in a town around Jacksonville. We had a good time for several days, then she wanted me to go out on a double date with her, or she couldn't go. I told her I was not old enough to date. She talked her parents into us taking a ride with her friend then he picked up another friend. They drove straight to a big Farm with lots of barns. The girl and her friend left me and the other friend there alone. I got out of the car I told the friend I was not old enough to date. He said okay, and we talked for a while. When they came back, her boyfriend asked the guy that was left with me if I was nice to him. He explained that I was not old enough to date.

Then her boyfriend jumped out of the car, told the guy in the back seat to hold me down, which he did. Then her boyfriend started touching me all over, trying to pull my pants off, kissing me, fought hard and just as he was going to contact my privates, his friend said no. Let her go! And he made the guy stop. The girl got mad at me and wouldn't talk to me for the rest of the week, and her mother didn't know why. I kept her secret. She was never my friend again. I asked to go home early. When I got home I did tell my mother about the whole trip.

My parents worked hard in the restaurant to make a living for all of us. The place brought so much sadness for all of us though. My parents were always having arguments, jealous of each other; I myself was always in the way. Let me tell you I had so many burns from being hit with a belt, all I had to do is walk up to my daddy and I got the belt across my legs, bottom, and the palm of my hands trying to stop the belt.

The situations that I learned, and experienced were bad. Seeing drunks suffocating in bowls of soup because they had too much to drink and passed out in their soup. Hearing/seeing persons talk about whom they just had sex with and coaxing others to go out back and try it out. Married couples fondling other person's wives or husbands. Hearing vulgar language constantly. Seeing my mother physically fight another woman over my daddy. My grandmother came to stay with us one time, so we wouldn't have to sit in the back room of the establishment and peel fifty- pound bags of potatoes on a Saturday night and could stay with her at home. She never came back again after some men came over to our house and want to pay for some services.

There is another situation that I still can't express to anyone from being in the living situation I was

. These were Disgusting and Shameful situations I had to endure. I don't blame my parents I ju
wanted to mention this so if you are in this situation with children PLEASE FIND A WAY TO GE
THE CHILDREN OUT OF IT. I know this has some bearing on why I've had a hard time with m
marriages and trusting anyone.

I have trouble letting anyone touch me, like putting hands on my shoulder, standing to close to me, c
getting in my face. I will step back and get in a full stance to be able to avoid any upcoming situation.
And I feel very uncomfortable when loud noises from others are raised, or even if the area I'm in hav
more than a couple of people around.

Always want to be able to get out of an area, never turn my back to anyone. When I sleep at night
someone walks into the room I immediately wake up and know someone is there. I feel them.

We lived in the forest with lots of springs and lakes around. From the time I was around ten as soc
as I got up I would go the springs and swim, get a small wood boat and take my dog patty and be c
the water for the whole day. Would sleep in the boat on the water, fish, just being by myself with th
beautiful sky, animals, and nature. Except for my children I have been a person that wants to be b
myself. I feel safer that way.

My parents knew I was okay because I knew how to swim. I was always a loner. I physically starte
getting better after we moved to the forest; the doctors said the spring water was helping me to hea

After that I was taken to my grandmother's home to live with her. I did love my grandmother, n
mother's mom. She was a simple person she was very nice to me she had long hair all the way down
her hips, she dyed it jet back, she was a full-figured woman and very pretty. I was always getting sic
I had to take three baths a day and use dial soap. I had bad sores on my legs and arms doctors said
was my blood problem.

I did feel like I was being sent away from my parents because they didn't want me around. My moth
would come see me every week if she could, it was only for a few minutes when she bought groceries f
the restaurant, but I didn't get to see my daddy. I missed him so much. I cried a lot because I could
see him. I always thought daddy didn't want to see me, my mother would say that he had to work ar
that he would come see me later.

After a while I would be able to visit my parents on weekends .

My daddy's mother visited me a lot she would bring us bags of food, because my grandma I lived wi
had no income. My daddy's mom worked and was always helping us. She was a great woman she alwa
took me to church, and Sunday Schools. She always talked to me and listened. Grandmother was ve
active in the community events. She made hats and had a good business. She was kind and showe
respect to the grandmother I lived with. The Church pastor preached about my parents one Sund
and I felt so bad and all the people there were looking at me didn't go back to church then. We we
to another church and the preacher came and visited us all the time.

I was blessed with two wonderful grandmothers, and both loved me, and always showed it wi their time and affection. I was close to both my grandmothers more than my mother for years. My grandmother that I lived with fried me liver in butter when I was real sick. The doctors said I needed it. It was so good she really showed a lot of affection and love to me. I was very blessed. When my son was born we had to have a lot of liver for him. Doctors' orders for around two years. My daddy would hunt deer for the liver.

My grandmother lived in the same house for years all her children were raised in the home. My great-grandmother lived there, grandfather, step grandfather, Aunts, Uncles.

At night I had a hard time sleeping in my room. I would always feel someone standing beside the right top part of the bed I slept in. It was the same bed my mother slept in when she was growing up. Steel bed with steel springs, just different mattress.

I could hear and feel them breathing real hard. I would cover up with the blanket pulled over my head and leave a little hole for me to breathe in air. In the summer time I was always very hot. I could feel several other persons in the room also. My grandmother was used to it.

She would put the dresser in front of the bedroom window I stayed in, and a dresser up against the front door in the living room where she slept. Chairs in front of the back door in the kitchen, aluminum pie plates in the hallway window, kitchen windows, and the front room where she slept. Glass milk bottles all over the kitchen floor, hallway, front room, and leave me a path to walk to the bathroom which had milk bottles and pie plates all on the floor except where the commode was for me to use.

Before dark, I would have to rake the yard up next to edge of the whole house where you would be able to see footprints if someone was to walk up to the house, and in front of the fence where the gate was, every day before it got dark

I would get so scared that I begged my grandmother to let me sleep with her. I only got to sleep with her two times that I can remember. The reason was her husband, my step grandfather told her never to let anyone else sleep in that bed. Only her. So that was why.

After I was older, I learned that my parents had split up and that was one of the major reasons I was sent elsewhere. That made me feel a little better, but I missed my family. I

My aunt and uncle came in from Texas, stayed with my grandmother, my cousin, and myself. That night my cousin slept on the living room couch. My aunt and uncle slept in my grandmother's bed, and grandmother slept on the couch in the hallway I slept in my room.

During the night my aunt and uncle were awakened for some reason. They started putting their pillows just in the right place and noticed on my aunt's pillow there was three letters written on the back of the pillow case in red. So, they woke everyone up.

My cousin, myself, grandmother, all of us. They accused all of us of writing the three letters on the pillowcase. After questioning they figured out none of us did it, we were all sound asleep during the time. So, they changed the pillowcase. By the way the letters were on the side against the mattress.

They woke up the next morning and there were three letters on the back of yet the second pillowcase, which was touching the mattress. E P A. My step -grandfathers initials are E.P.A. – Edgar Poe Anderson. They took both pillowcases to the local FBI agency and had the writing analyzed. They could not figure out what the substance was it was not ink, crayons, etc. IT WAS RED IN COLOR.

After that, everyone wanted to know who had died in the house. Well did I find out some information that really made me start to understand why I always felt someone breathing? 1. Grandfather, 2. Great-Grandmother, 3. Baby Uncle Homer, 4. Step-Grandfather. (EPA)

I wet the bed until early teen years, my mother would get me back by putting the mattress out in front of the yard for everyone to see. I tried to put the mattress in the back yard, but she wouldn't have it. She wanted everyone around to know about it. Several years later I learned my daddy's step brother was beaten also for wetting the bed, my grandmother hid it from his daddy a lot so he wouldn't get a beating for it no matter how we tried we couldn't help it, I wet the bed until I was around thirteen I woke up starting to so I would fall out of the bed and make it outside or to the bathroom. Some things are meant to be.

My parents had always fought, I mean really fought. My mother would argue with my dad all the time.

She pushed him, hit him, he would walk away from her, but she just kept on following him. Until finally each time there would be a fight. One time in our kitchen my mother's body went thru the sheetrock wall and you could see the way she entered the wall arms up legs out the whole sculpture of her body was very detailed.

My mama didn't want him to change it, so she could show it to everyone who came over. They loved each other but boy did they argue. I figured out after I was grown up that the only reason they were together was because in those days people didn't get divorced, they had to grin and bear it.

Any time my parents went out on the town with their friends they would always get jealous over each other talking to others, or dancing with others. They would argue and fight for days

Mama always broke our plates, dishes, cups she would be mad and throw them at my daddy, and me. Mama seemed to be two different people, to people not living at home with us she was real nice, quiet, pleasant. At home she was always mad. Mama pulled a butcher knife one day in the kitchen we were standing in front of each other she had raised the knife up to stab someone I walked by and saw it, and I ran in the kitchen grabbed her arm and knocked the knife out of her hand I was around twelve or thirteen.

I remember my mother telling me, she was sitting in the dining room, brushing my hair. You know if it wasn't for you your daddy and I would be just fine. My mother's temper was short, one day we were going down the road and she got mad at me I was around fourteen or fifteen, she reached over my lap opened the car door and tried to push me out while the car was going. As soon as she relieved her tension she seemed to be okay then took me to school. I loved my mother, but she was very unpredictable, I was always on guard. When my mother was seventy-one she got mad at me for letting some water drops stay on the stainless-steel sink she got a big knife and chased me into the back room. She kept hitting the door for me to let her in, I said no, I kept it locked and after a couple hours she was fine. I was very cautious when I went out.

I saw my daddy hit my mother after she hit him several times, he was not supposed to hit her, but she just lost it, and was a different person when she attacked him. The only way it stopped was for him to hit her one time then she would stop.

Once, my mother had left for two weeks, I kept asking daddy when mama was coming home. He kept saying, don't worry I'll always take care of you it will be okay. She came back she had been gone off with another person. The next day she came back home from the doctor with a neck brace.

The last time she tried to hit me I grabbed her arm and told her if she ever tried to hit me again I would hit her back. I had my two-year old daughter on my hip.

When I was around twelve we all moved back in together after around a year to a lakefront home. Daddy fixed it up real nice. I had a room, so did my parents. It was right on the lake, I stayed in the lake on a boat all the time there too. We would swim with the gators, you could shine a light on the top of the water right where we swam and could see the gators there with you.

At that time the gators were still scared of man, not now they will kill you.

I was afraid of my daddy, he was quick tempered, we had to wake him up with a broom or we would get hit from him waking up. He was on guard from the war he was hurt several times with ammo. He called it JUMPIE, so we always made a lot of noise when we came up to him, so he would know it was his kids coming.

I really loved my daddy and when he passed away I wanted to die. I loved and respected him. When I got married and had children he was so happy to have grandchildren.

I made sure he got to see them all the time.

My mother didn't really want to see too much of my children only on holidays when daddy was here, after that she didn't until she got in her seventies, then she wanted me around all the time, but was never satisfied with anything I ever did. She would let me know all the time. But, when she needed something, or wanted company she would expect me to be there. I treated my mother with respective, and always showed her love. Sometimes we argued mostly I would leave so it wouldn't get so bad, her favorite words were 'YOUR JUST LIKE YOUR DADDY – I SEE YOUR DADDY WHEN YOU WALK IN THE DOOR".

After my daddy was deceased my mother called me over to her house one day and asked me to take her new bed frame out of the house. I asked why she said only you would understand, but last night I was touched by someone in this bed trying to make love to me. I told her I had heard of that before and that I understood. So, I got the bed out of the house. There was someone attached to the bed. She was at least 60 years old at that time. I just knew!!!

As I stated before I have always been a loner, the only person I could really talk to be my daddy of which I feared, or my grandmother which I trusted with all my heart.

Daddy had a boat with a small motor that I used when I wasn't in school. I would go out on the lake all day and just stay on the water. I felt safe on the water. The only thing I had to worry about were snakes that would sometimes try to come into the boat that were very poisonous. By this time my dog patty was gone she had to live with my grandmother because the gators kept trying to get her so daddy gave her to my grandmother to take care of for her safety.

I would stay on the water for hours not going in until just before dark. At this age I started having different kinds of pictures as I called them. I had to be outside of the house not enclosed inside.

I always have known what other people were thinking, and if they were not telling the truth or not. Or if someone was mean inside and putting on for others as being real nice since I was little. After I got older I started remembering things that happened.

When I was around 12-14 years old. I tried to fly. I would start running and flap my arms and try to fly. Jumped off high places and tried to fly. I just felt it was something I was to do. Sounds stupid doesn't it. I JUST WANTED TO GET OUT OF HERE.

When I remember things it's like a movie in fast motion. This is one of them: Always black and white – no color. Until my sixty's.

I was in the boat on the water and there seems to be a lot of wind above me. The water was swirling around the boat. The wind woke me up I had on a short sleeve white shirt and a pair of multi-colored knee shorts. No shoes. My hair was short and curly.

I saw something above and I couldn't make out what it was because it was so wide and low to the water, it looked flat, there was a circular hole that I was being lifted to while I was still laying down. I was then on this cold stainless-steel floor that was like a circular stopper flush to where the whole was. There were others standing at the ends of the circular piece of stainless steel around me. They looked like small children, but they didn't look like I did.

These beings were short had two legs and two arms and were covered with a smock like dress. No shoes. No toes. No mouth. No hair. No ears. Didn't notice their hands. I did notice their eyes, kind of round and slanted at the same time. Skin looked like soft gray, and soft rubber or elastic.

I stood up and one of the beings was talking to me within my head. The others were just touching me, and I could hear their giggles, and their excitement of meeting me. I was not scared at all, I felt great. Like I was part of them, or at home, or had seen them before, I wasn't worried.

I looked forward and saw a circular room in front of me. There were all types of instruments there with lights. Real tall beings (3) were working the instruments while standing up. There were a lot of symbols on the instruments. Recognized the symbols when I saw them, they looked like Egyptian writings. The beings that were standing had real long arms and white hoods over their heads. The fingers were long with long hairs and their heads were long, wide and different. They looked kind of like tan lizards sounds funny don't it.

High above the instrument room I could see a circular room with a balcony like area and different types of beings were sitting around the round balcony with different type colored hoods. I could not see all the beings just a couple that looked like the one using the instruments. I could not see the top of the room it was too dark.

As I turned back to the small beings around me still an older one came up to me and without talking asked me to follow her. This one was the same as the first ones except she had brown hair that was the page cut style.

We started walking down the circular wall. As we walked the children started to disappear into the right wall until there was myself, and the one being with the hair and I noticed I was on a type of metal bed with a thin mattress that was pushed up against the wall. I could see the hallway going both ways in a circle, she was standing right beside me on the left. I was starting to ask what was wrong. Why am I on this bed, she kept answering don't be afraid.

Then I woke up and notice I was in a room where a lot of (people) were around me. I felt safe. I could not see anyone's face. I saw a round tube in my stomach where my navel was. There was an orange fluid going into my stomach.

It was a huge room. Lots of beings around me, the orange fluid was going in and coming out for some time.

I woke up in the boat that I had been out in all day until just before dark. I did not know what had happened to me I just thought I been asleep all day. But, I did not have a sun- burn on that day. I should have been red as a beet. I was 13 years old.

I saw this at least twenty-years later during regression. It's like a fast movie along with many others that have happen to me during this life. Was told by my parents that I was no longer sick when I got to be around 14 or 15 years of age.

I often ask myself why I wasted so many years and not realize what has been going on.

Why didn't I pay attention to my choices?

Or maybe / are my choices decided before I came?

Why couldn't I listen earlier in my life?

Why couldn't I see before now?

I've been praying since I can remember, I've always known others were around me, watching me. I have seen some real ugly animals, and people before just standing by the road as we would drive by. My daughter and I saw a man in front of us one night like he didn't want us to go forward, she didn't top, he was in black and had real torn clothes on his face was all dark looking we didn't slow down when we approached the exact spot in front of us he was gone.

When I graduated from school I got married. Loved this man more than anything else in the world. Except for God. I was a good wife, I tried to get pregnant, and I don't know if you know of this one even had a false pregnancy. I went to the doctors they said I was pregnant. Body acted pregnant.

NO Baby. I gained weight stomach got larger, morning sickness. NO BABY.

I kept my dog a Saint Bernard with me; he protected me. One night I was crying so hard and upset and suddenly I felt a hand slowly touch my leg and I stopped crying and wasn't upset any more I knew God had answered my prayers.

One day I was asked to swap partners by some friends told them to get out of my house.

Well here we go again:

Several times I've visited places a place where. I've seen children that look human but are not all human the eyes are colored different; the round face and heads are perfectly round. Communicate with eyes no voices. Only after I started, and my children started seeing vessels did I get introduced to the different babies and children. Certain females are used for breeding special children and never know it. Develop must faster and mothers don't even know. Babies are taken much faster than 40 years ago.

Approximately two years later I went to the doctor and the doctor did a surgical procedure on me. Within two weeks I was pregnant. Within three weeks after that I was alone he decided he didn' want a baby he just wanted me. I said no way!!! I will not harm this baby, he left. We had been going to church together, planning together, etc. So, I went forward.

Started having a lot of strange things happens around me after the baby was born.

By the way I named him "Michael" after Archangel Michael. When Michael was born I had a hard time. I was paralyzed from the waist down for several days, and then I just dragged one leg for about six months after using the electrical charges to my leg. After around two years my leg got okay. I still have a lot of problems from having the surgery to get the baby out of my body and not hurt him. God saved both of us that day.

I was twenty-three I stayed with my parents at night I could always feel someone in the room. Someone that made me uneasy, my son was a big boy he weighed ten pounds and five ounces when he was born so I put him in bed with me, I just couldn't leave him alone in the baby bed. One night I kept feeling someone at the end of the bed I set up and saw a man standing there with a black robe on, a black hat and eyes that appeared red/orange colored. I ordered it to be gone in the name of Jesus and never return

A few nights later I was in bed and on my right side, my arm was hanging off the bed Someone was pulling my arm trying to pull me off the bed, and I really mean pulling hard enough to wake me up Again, I ordered him to be gone in the name of Jesus

Several weeks after that a woman named Nina called me and wanted me to come and meet her that she had heard I was with child. I responded yes and asked her to explain her phone inquiry. She wanted to meet me because she had been done the same way to her as this man had done to me. I agreed to meet her at her mother's home because she was very sick.

I met her, and she was very sick with Lupus her daughter was around two years old, and Nina and her mother were very nice. I asked her to go to church with me and she started church before she passed away and was baptized.

After several times being around Nina before she passed one night I started telling her about the man I saw at my bed one night. She interrupted me and said let me tell you what he looked like, and who he was. She described the man perfectly, and said it is his father. He had been described to her before.

I had thought myself that my mother was the one sending the negative images because of her not wanting anyone in the house with her and daddy. Daddy wanted us there.

He went and had air-conditioning put in the house before my son and I came home from the hospital, and that made my mother furious that he did that for us.

Me, my son and daddy got along good in the house, I cleaned the house up, cooked, washed clothes to help. Mama had wanted me to not have the baby, she asked me in front of Daddy if I was going to keep the baby and before I had a chance to answer

Daddy said why of course she is. So, I figured I need to get my own place because not only was I in the way so was my baby.

Later, in my years around 50 my mother told me she was forced to get an abortion by daddy and his mother. I felt kind of sorry for her having to do that, in the 40's women didn't have too many choices. My parents grew up during the hard depression. My daddy's parents were a lot better off than my mother's family. Mama had six siblings with only her mother to take care of them. They had no help and had to scrap for food and clothing. I could read my mother's feelings all the time.

So, finally I got a nice small trailer and parked it on daddy's property. Right after I moved in Michael was very sick I went to the doctor's office weekly. My son had been sick we were in bed it was storming outside bad. The lights were off it was storming so badly something kept banging on the wall of the trailer right where we were sleeping, I mean like someone taking a fist and hitting the wall only in one spot. I felt pure evil/negativity outside. I'm not a spooky type of person either. I could feel it strongly.

I was praying so hard then I fell to sleep and was woken up with the brilliant Shining light at the side of the bed with a being. I was told to take my son away from there to someone who could help him. Then it was gone. I checked my baby and I could tell he had gotten worse. I took him to the hospital they admitted him. He was in the hospital for several days.

Mike and I got married and he fell in love with my son.

We were married for seventeen years: Lived together for 14.

Mike, I, and our son were happy when our daughter came she is a beautiful black haired, brown eyed girl. He worked, I worked we visited our parents and went to church.

I saw Mike's uncle's house in Virginia and described it to him and told him someone is going to pass away from there. Couple days later his Uncle died. I had never been there.

I saw Mike's mother at my bed before she died she came and visited. Told him to go and visit her before she left. She died a few days after.

Mike started drinking daily, myself I was trying to survive and take care of the children.

Always praying, trying to live right and having a hard time not being emotional about the drinking and the expense of Mike doing so. One-night Mike called me into the bathroom and told me someone was just talking to him and said he was going to take our son away from him. I rebuked the evil/negativity never to return.

My daddy died on January 18th, 1985, Mike's daddy died two weeks later.

We were no help to each other emotionally for ourselves or our children.

Here we go again:

During this time my son, my daughter, and myself witnessed several flying objects around our living area we witness three individual flying objects a little above the trees.

They all started going upward and two individually went into the first one. Then the first one, which had the other two go in went straight upward out of our sight. I went home and called the local County Sheriff's Office and she said it's nothing, at the same time two jets went over our house just a few feet from the top of our trees. I said oh really then what are the jets doing up there!

Several times I have woken up and there would be bright lights all around our dwelling especially where the wooded area was. I would wake up, but I could not move. I couldn't talk or move my arms or legs. I could see someone standing outside the window looking in and they were tall. The lights were real bright, and everything was silent.

I remember being carried out to a vehicle it was real bright in the wooded area in the back of the house on a flat surface, and my son was being carried out also.

I could see he was asleep, I didn't see my daughter anywhere.

Several times I could see the hallway with the bright lights and movement, but I could not move. My son would see the lights also. It was when my daughter got older that she would see the lights at another residence then she would know what was going on but couldn't move.

We maintained our church attendance for spiritual strength and guidance, started receiving assistance from church for groceries. My salary would not pay for everything community friends would help with groceries. Mike could not hold a job because of the drinking, emotional outburst, and driving record he left the scene of several vehicle accidents.

Saw my Daddy at his bed one night during January 1985, he turned around and looked at me, he was reading something out of a book, but the funny thing was my Daddy was in the living room with around 15 other people. Daddy died a few days later.

My daddy died, I was devastated my children were devastated we were all so close.

Ten days later Mike's daddy died. My daddy had always told me Sandy if I'm alive you will have a place to stay and food to eat when I'm gone you're on your own.

I was numb. My heart felt like someone was putting a knife in it and twisting it all the time. I knew I had to get my children out of the environment we were in or they would not have a chance. I prayed, I prayed, I prayed, I prayed. Constantly.

Currently Mike was starting to really get out of control. Drunk all the time. Not working. Catching the bed and himself on fire. Catching my gown on fire several times from smoking in the bed. All his monies he did make went to the bar at the end of each week sometimes it got as high as $600.00. I was trying to hold on to a man for the family that was not holy.

I would say terrible words cuss, holler, and not acting like myself. When I walked into our residence all I saw was a door with nothing but darkness inside. Mike started arguments with my son he physically tried to hurt my son with a hammer.

I became someone I am not. I became physical and defended my son, daughter, and myself. We were in a corner, my son and daughter behind me:

Mike was coming towards us to hurt us all. There was a table in front of us that took three men to get into the dining room. As Mike came towards us I stepped out and picked up the table and threw it across the room on top on him. We left the evil at that time. I knew that I had listen to God at that moment and with God's protection we had broken away from the evil. My son, daughter and I got into the vehicle outside and left.

Asked God where to go. I got a phone call after we left and was told to go a house and stay there for three month. A stranger called at the appropriate time.

One of God's strangers not family, friends, a stranger! I trusted the trust and God has taken care of me since!!!!!!

Negativity was still trying to hold us down I had started to make the right choices and trust God. I wanted to keep my family unit so bad I would not let my programming go. I let go and Let God.

I didn't know where we were going, how I was going to take care of my children.

I just knew God would take care of everything. He Did and Continues to.

Here we go again:

We found a house and moved in, after a couple of weeks we all notice the bathroom toilet would flush at night with no-one in there. My daughter and son noticed it first and told me then I noticed. The room I slept in was nice with the furniture from the last resident.

She had passed away some years ago and her husband had just passed away in a nursing home facility. One morning I woke up and my daughter asked me how I cut my gown on my back.

I looked, and it looked like I had cut it with a straight cut at an angle. I didn't pay much attention to it. The next night I wore the same gown with the original cut on top. The next morning, I got up and the gown had been cut not torn all the way across the back of the gown in a different place.

So, I figured someone was trying to get my attention. So, I asked the person we were renting from what was the lady's name that lived there before and had passed away.

(Boy was I scared, just thinking I would be able to communicate with someone whom had passed away. What was wrong with me!!!!)

Landlord Said Barbara, so that night I sat in the room on the bed and verbally asked if Barbara wanted to speak to me. She started telling me that she didn't mind us there but the person who took care of her husband had stolen a lot of things and made him sign a power of attorney form. But, she was very angry that all her nic knacks (figures like animals, glasses, people collect) were sold and she wanted her daughters to get most of them and she wanted me to tell her about the crystal light that she stole. To confront her and let her know that Barbara knows and is not happy.

NOW THAT'S WHEN I STARTED THINKING SANDY WHAT IS GOING ON HERE. ARE YOU OKAY!!!!!! There was no voice just like thought patterns went through my head, real clear.

The lady was to come by on the next day to get the rent.

When she came I gave her the rent and told her I had something to tell her.

That I have a message for you. She said what's the message. I told her exactly what Barbara had told me. She looked at me and said did you know Barbara? I stated no. She asked how to do you know about the items you're referring to. I stated Barbara came to me and asked me to ask you and tell you that she is not happy about the power of attorney papers, but especially the knic knacks.

She said there is no way you could have known about the crystal lights. She told me to move immediately, that she was selling the house and wants her maintenance man to stay there until it sold. She feared Barbara.

I informed her at that time how the toilet flushes at night by itself, and that someone of the spirit world that hasn't left this house yet is living in the laundry room, because he always touches Michael at night and keeps him awake. (My son had been telling me of the man in the room)

After that we moved into my friend's house. We stayed about two months. All three of us would end up in the living room right after we would go to bed in the three rooms.

My daughter could feel a presence, my son couldn't sleep in his room, and I could not breathe in the room I was in. So, every night we slept on the couch or floor in the living room. One night we were watching television and my son looked up and saw a man walk down the hall. He said Mama is someone else in the house, I answered no.

He said a man with a tee shirt and work pants just walked down the hall and looked at me. So, I called my friend and asked her to come down. My son told her what he saw she said that sounds like my dad. He always wore his tee shirts and long work pants in the house. I asked her do we have your permission to be here. She said yes, I asked her to please let whoever was there to know. She verbally told her dad, mom, and anyone else there that we had her permission to be there. After that we still slept in the living room.

CAN YOU IMAGINE ME, AROUND FORTY SOMETHING, MY SON AROUND 16, AND MY DAUGHTER AROUND 14 EXPERIENCING THESE THINGS? WELL WE STUCK TOGETHER. IF ONE HAD A PROBLEM WE ALL HAD A PROBLEM.

WE ALL THREE KNEW GOD WAS TAKING CARE OF US AND WE TRUSTED IN HIM TOTALLY.

By the way: Wherever we went Barbara came.

Barbara led me to a house where she had lived before. I remembered playing out in the front yard with some other kids when I was little. The streets were not paved at that time. Eventually Barbara went back to that house.

Here we go again:

In our next house my son had a little Blonde girl in his room he got to know. I felt her presence but never saw her. Barbara always played jokes on Jackie. Jackie didn't want to acknowledge Barbara but on several occasions, Jackie would call me and ask me to have Barbara please put her car keys back on the counter so she could go to work, that her keys were on the counter a few minutes ago and now they're gone. My daughter would call back and say okay she put them back.

Christmas time: My daughter and I were in front of the Christmas tree and all the bulbs started moving back and forth at once. It scared my daughter, it didn't bother me, and I figured it was the little girl.

Here we go again:

I was approached by several dark energies and had to really protect myself;

I woke up several times and my son would be standing by my bed with a bat, had several candles lit and I asked what was wrong he would say I feel evil around and I'm protecting us all.

I woke up one night and saw a man standing by the bed reading a bible facing the window. I knew this man from another time. He wore clothes from the 18th Century.

DO ANY OF YOU UNDERSTAND WHY I'M WRITING THIS!!

THERE IS NOTHING WRONG WITH ME, MY SON OR MY DAUGHTER.

Or You!!!!!

There's a reason I had a lot of drama when I was little.

There is a reason why both children had drama experiences and now have attunement with sensitivity to different energies!!

We must concede, grant, allows God to be within our total essence.

God's plan is just that.

Here we go again:

My daughter and I moved into an apartment several nights after moving around twenty-miles away from where we had lived for around sixteen years the lights started back. My daughter noticed them first, she told me the lights were back and outside her window. It seemed wherever I was the lights came. I noticed the light several times myself and prayed for my daughter and myself. I would ask for the crafts to take me instead of my daughter.

I was having a lot of very intense nose - bleeds for a while, the doctors couldn't figure out why. I would pass out at work for no reasons, I was able to feel it coming on.

I had to have some test done in the hospital twice I was asked when I had surgery on the left side my head. I stated I haven't both times the nurses said to me oh yes you have the scars, the indention above the ears. Nosebleeds stopped after these tests.

The doctors put me in a hospital for five days and wired my head up with glue, no one has ever told me anything. They were measuring the brain activity to make sure I didn't have any strokes they said. No records were ever given to me.

I was going down the road to meet some friends one night with another friend in the car. I started feeling something around the car; no lights were anywhere, no noise, the passenger started noticing no cars behind us but lights on top of us. I figured it was the crafts again she was scared bad. The lights where there but no vehicle was visible.

We made it to the eatery place.

I started going to some meetings to learn what in the world was going on with me. I see, feel, talk to spirits, see lights and crafts, what is going on. Am I the only one, my children are seeing them too. But, usually when they are around with me.

I started reading books on metaphysical subjects around my late forties.

My son (19), my daughter (16) and myself were in Tennessee one night and my son woke me up he turned the lights on. He had red marks all over this chest/shoulders, arms, and face someone had been hitting him. I rebuked the evil/negativity then my son got in the bed with where I was. I went to bed where he was sleeping and nothing else happened. I asked the owner if anyone had died in that room, he said why something bothering you. He wouldn't give us a different room. I could feel something in the room. After I prayed it left us alone.

Then these cars were following me all the time, blue cars, I would go to the flea market and notice the same drivers of the cars would be standing right where I was. One of my closest friends had helped a lot of people in his life time I figured it was him they were watching.

He helped me to accept the changes that were occurring in my life's path. He's been gone for several years now, and then it was black trucks, or white cars. Sometimes they still are right behind me. I'm talking about going on small trips.

So now does any of this sound familiar to you, have you been experiencing any of these circumstances?

The last time I went on a trip around 100 miles one way myself and another passenger were on the correct road heading the correct way, the same road we came by. Then the passenger asked where is Crystal River? I answered on the West Coast.

She said we are only a few miles from there according to that sign. We did not get lost.

We lost around 45 minutes and were heading the wrong direction when we notice it.

I was in a relationship and would ride from home to my destination and leave around nine and not get home until around three hours later and I was going the same route all the time. My partner was going to notify the sheriff's office to see if I had been in an accident. The same thing happens a lot. So now I write down the time, so I can tell if I've lost time. The longest time lost was around three hours. My family was getting ready to call the highway patrol because I was only 30 minutes from home. I left home only five miles from a meeting one night and I got to the meeting an hour later as everyone was leaving.

Here we go again:

I have been visited by Angel beings with a lot of children with them. I was to speak to each of the children to encourage them before taking off to another realm of existence.

I really enjoyed that I love children.

I visited a woman in Gainesville she asked me to come and see the vortex in her dwelling and to communicate with the beings outside of her home. Didn't know this older woman only that at several crystal shops she did charts for others well respected by community. I noticed an opening of energy in the room swirling so I closed it. Then I saw five figures outside very tall non-human in their spirit-multi-dimensional bodies they wanted to leave this plane, so I asked my creator to assist and then they were gone. You could feel the wind as they left. Few weeks later she called for assistance again, at that time I could feel a childlike figure buried under her concrete steps, sent the entity to Father/Mother God and Jesus for the child's future placement.

One night I was asleep and was awaken by a voice that said get up and go south. This voice was not out loud it was like a fact inside my thought patterns. I got up it was around 4:00 am I had no money and little gas. I got in my car and went south. I came up on this small town around forty miles away there were three stores there. For some reason I knew it was where I was supposed to be. There was a furniture store open, so I walked into the store. A woman in the center of the store behind a round desk said "Well it's about time I 've been praying all night for someone to come or I was going to kill myself" I spoke up and said I'm here and visited and spoke with her and said whatever God told me to say. So, after some time I left, and I did make it home on any empty tank. I obeyed.

Recently I was going to another town when I was told to stop at the next store and go in.

So, I stopped I didn't want to stop but I did, I walked around inside the store didn't see anyone or anything that I felt was to be paid attention to and walked back to my car and started going where I was going. I heard a voice say JUST WANTED TO SEE IF YOU ARE LISTENING.

Instant Movie: Several Years Back.

I was walking through some doors into an operating room I had gown on I don't know how I looked, but it was me.

I saw human bodies on the left side of the room that had been drained of liquids / backbone was taken out of each one of them from the neck to the tailbone. These bodies still had their original clothes own except for the torn parts.

These bodies were from different parts of the world. A lot of them were from rural areas and in good shape medically. Humans that wouldn't be missed as much as some others. These bodies were to be destroyed.

On the right side of the room were tables with beings placing the backbones completely into similar looking humans. These similar looking humans were not alive yet. There were tables and tables of them. I was ordered out.

I started noticing animal spirits around 50 years old. Black panther, White Doves, and the most interesting was the Cobra it was beautiful. (I have always been terrified of snakes) I was very sick woke up looking at Mother Mary, Jesus, and the Cobra with awesome colors of blue. After their visit I started getting well just the essence of them being there healed me. Right before I woke up I was hanging on two types of wires in a real big hanger like place with a lot of other people hanging the same way. The wires were under my legs at the knees and under my arms at my shoulder.

*Seen several beings on the roads that really aren't there in this realm.

*Noticing structures that aren't physically there.

*One looked like a huge dog coyote at least five feet tall sitting by a tree when I first moved to the SW area.

*Or people standing on the side of the road to distract you.

*Looked into co-worker's eyes and noticed their pupils looked like a cat's pupils up/down at first glance.

I have left this plane before and returned several times. I was in a coma for fourteen days

I remember seeing crafts above the building, the stars, and I completely woke up set up in a void plane where nothing was moving, no noise, no stars, nothing, no wind, at first, I felt fear, then I remember saying I'll just go back for a while.

These are just some of the things that have occurred during the past 52 years of my life here on planet earth. 1948 - 2000.

Since 2001 I have conceded to doing whatever Father/Mother God sends me to do.

Being a servant of all is being on call.

I have owned material items, land, cars, jewelry, and a secure job. Three times I was told to get rid of material items and be on call for services needed for others by spirit.

To serve God: not man and to let go of programming.

Prestige will not make you happy in the long run.

Gossip / Judgment, towards others is Fear.

Having a personal relationship with someone is rare, unless you find someone like yourself that isn't ashamed of being whomever they are. Lots of times even your immediate family will walk away from you- afraid of other persons perceptions.

For a long time, I just couldn't call myself a Psychic. Man has put the labels on us.

Never felt worthy - Psychic Counseling – Sandra Marie – Humble – Messenger -

**Webster's Dictionary indicates:**

**PSYCHIC means;**

Analytic, intelligent, psychological, spiritual, telepathic, mystic, immaterial.

**PHENOMENON means;**

Fact, experience, happening

**UNUSUAL means;**

It's your service. Each individual Universal Spiritual Being is unique!!

I make mistakes I'm a Universal Spiritual Being in a human physical body.

**Well this is up to 2000.**

2001 to present is very different from what I've shared so far.

Introduced by Spirit, Quartz Crystals, and Rocks.

a Photos: Colors of my energy surrounding my body.

ite are spiritual energies assisting with awareness. Blue are calming energies of love and pea
nge colors are energies that I've been around other persons assisting them with their spiritual ne
ch attach to myself until I release them. Green is healing energies from myself showing hea
itually. Red is passion for life and spiritual love..

Plasma: spiritual beings

Plasma energy outside with my family children and grandchildren. Spiritual beings around us

Aura photo shows energy around my body with spiritual assistance from beings of love and light.

Me and my daughter in Arizona.

was living in the country had a nice piece of land and working at my job, both kids were married and on their own. Going to different places to learn about new things going on around me that I was noticing. At work I had to be careful not to let others see me go to the phone and pick it up before it rang and watch not to hand files to my supervisor before he had asked me for them. Little things I'd notice I had to not respond to. Some of the workers in the office would notice even when I tried not to be noticed. At my residence located around fifteen miles South of main town it was very apparent that were trees around the whole area that had the tops burned down from something burning / hitting the tops. I could feel the movement of aircraft during the nights and when it was cloudy rainy days. Never heard anything just could feel the movement. Saw a large craft that appeared to be going down at an angle to land, along with the other craft that raced in front of it, there was another person in a truck front of me that stopped and stood outside his vehicle and we watched them both at the same time it was before dark. After that day I decided to sell my place and move closer into town away from the forest. Even though I knew what I saw I just didn't feel comfortable in the woods any more especially with the coyotes being there. I was visited by a lot of spiritual beings, some our body type and some totally different from other dimensions. Lots of lights were always outside my residence the coyotes ate a lot of the neighbor dogs, and cats. The land around me had governmental signs NO Trespassing!! All the neighbors were aware what was going on.

So, I moved into town into an apartment right down from where I worked.

I started getting a lot of visitors at night wanting to talk to me. (Spirits) I couldn't see them, but I knew someone was there. I kept this information to myself until I went to a priest at a Catholic Church. I was raised Southern Baptist. I didn't know what to say, I felt so intimidated by him, but he was very understanding. He was so patient with me I kept calling him preacher. He made me feel welcome after a few minutes had gone by, I asked him was I going crazy or was evil trying to take over. After, I told him what had been going on with me he told me this. Sandy sounds to me like you've being contacted by heavenly beings, and God has chosen you to do special things for others and a lot of times people don't listen, but you have chosen to listen. Evil is not in you, your being guided by God. After that I felt much better about the things that I had been going thru. I have always been able to understand what spirits are trying to tell me, I have always had to have a fan, air conditioner, some type of noise to block out the spirit words, it's like a bunch of people talking at once. When one spirit is sharing the others quite down. It was very hard working in a place that mistreated employees that worked under them. One day I noticed one of supervisor's pupils were like a cat, yes just like a cat. That was weird. I had heard of that before, and that explained her actions. Everyone seemed to like me, and people were always nice to me except the evil ones that were on power trips. I could feel their reasoning and anger at certain employees that wouldn't stand up for themselves. I did stand up for myself, and others and would document things said, actions done, etc. This always made me a target because I always looked out for everybody. It was several years later but every one of those evil persons received their just reward Karma works, and I mean sometimes we see it sometimes we don't, but it works eventually.

Aura photo after several readings. Energy from others tries to join mine. Some vampire energies.

I started going to classes in Gainesville, instructor as I now understand a very highly Advanced Master of Enlightenment. He has assisted so many persons with guidance, assistance, and so many levels of enlightenment. One of his quotes was: "It Is What It Is". I met many other gifted persons in his classes. I now understand what he used to say about all your perceptions, visions and understandings of life will help you begin to concede to your new perceptions of Higher Awareness, Acknowledgment of the true Source of Life. I when I was younger I referred to God as "God". For years now, I open my praise and prayer with Father / Mother God and Jesus. The Divine Creator.

I lost a lot of time when I'd travel to Gainesville. So, I started writing down the time I left and that's how I verified my lost time. Sometimes it was one-three hours lost. I could tell when it started, there was always these two lights in front of me level to each other. weather was usually wet and damp. I was doing a lot of reading s while holding different crystals.

People would come back or call and let me know / or verify the readings. I was always afraid of telling people the wrong things, I never knew what I said, only spirit and the person receiving the messages. Since 2001 my energies have changed. It's like I'm always tuned in to whatever is going on.

Mother was still here then she seemed to need me around her more, she would come and visit me for lunch and I spent a lot of time with her when I was off work. She started sharing things with me she had never shared before, about phenomenon that had been going on around her all her life. She shared the bedroom experiences she and her brothers had in the room I used to sleep in at her mother's home. The reason she did was because of the meetings, and seminars I was going to all the time to learn more about spiritual enlightenment and phenomenon. When I would go to classes I would meet new people that I enjoyed being around and we would share out experiences. During this period, I started having real bad nose bleeds, the doctors couldn't figure out why. I was tested several times. I was admitted to Shands for testing, never told anything, never received a bill. Hush, Hush by my doctor. My brain waves were interesting to the Doctors at Shand's was all he shared. I was getting visions all the time, mainly about children, I would see babies in their mother's wombs, one time I was so upset, when I stood in front of her the baby seemed black dead. I couldn't stand it I went to the mother's house and asked to see her daughter that I had something to share with her. I was so sick all over, I wanted to help, the mother said she's not here, I emphasized I needed to see her, the mom spoke up and said, she went and had an abortion this morning, I was devastated, sick at my stomach, like I was grieving. It made me happy when I felt babies that were already being loved by their parents.

I started knowing when someone was physically sick, I'd notice the part of their body that was diseased. But, I never shared unless the person asked me. It could have changed their whole life experience and provided fear. One time I was in a restaurant this man was sitting behind me, I kept feeling an urgency to say hello to him. So, as I started to leave I turned around and said hello, he spoke back and started talking to me, said he hadn't felt good all day, I asked him if I could share something with him, he said yes. Well, I said I want you to leave here and go to the doctor, it's extremely important, he said okay your right something is wrong, I said do you promise, he said right now I'm going, my chest is not feeling right. I said you'll be okay, just drop everything and go now. He smiled and said, Thank You,

My aura picture: Very happy and peaceful.

One of the nursing home called the day we buried my Mother a man had wondered out of the nursing home, staff asked me to help and see where he had been, so she faxed a picture of him to me, I held the picture, and in my thought patterns I could see him on a Road with the road numbers, the type of vehicle he was in, the young man trying to help him, they found him on the side of the road where I sent them. Another time they wanted me to come and visit a man that was dying. So, I said okay, I walked in his room.

This is what I saw! His spirit body was white sitting up from his physical body, he said hello, and was smiling so big, he was so happy! He went up, and he shared that with me. It was awesome.

stayed with my mother for a few months and she had a lot of breakdowns, she would get so mad at me if I walked into the room, and chase after me with a butcher knife, or if I got water on the stainless-steel sink. She would lock up her bedroom door to make sure no one went into her room. She got paranoid about most things. She started trying to hit me again along with the knives I would just go into my room and let her calm down for several hours. That was the pattern she and daddy had. She would make me keep my groceries separate from hers, little things meant a lot to her. So, I got my own place and checked on her every day until she got real sick. When I did get my own apartment, she came over one night and demanded several cans of beans, said I stole them when I moved, she really embarrassed her boyfriend, I was okay from her actions. I gave her all my can goods. She was happy then. She liked being in control, that was another reason mother was always mad at me, I would listen and then do as I pleased, my son was all boy, I backed him up, stuck with him, mother wanted me to put him in a reform school, I said no, I will take care of him, and teach him to be a good Christian and man. I stuck with him, and I'm proud of him. He also is a servant of our Divine God, so Is my daughter, I'm proud of her too. I was given the privilege to be Divine's children mother. I was truly blessed. I always put Divine first, children second because I knew God Divine would take care of us. I made the choice of Jesus when my I was told to choose my family or Jesus, I said no choice, I choose Jesus.

I really miss my mother she was nicer to me the last two years of her life than she ever was before. She would call me on Saturday mornings and say where are you I've been waiting on you to pick me up and go to the store. I would spend the whole day going where she wanted. Garage sales, the last time I took her she said I'm going to get a new boyfriend today. When she came out of the store she a phone number and pointed out the new boyfriend. mother was a beautiful woman.

I was always on defense I never knew what would happen with my mother. She just didn't know why she was very jealous of me.

My mother got real sick with cancer I knew she was going to leave I felt it. She had surgery and they told us she only had a few weeks and they wanted to keep her on breathing machines. So, she was on them for around a month and I knew she didn't want that, so I asked the doctor to take her off because of her living will. The doctor told us no that she could live without it, so I told him to take her off if she could live without it.

I was there when they took the breathing machine off she had it off about five minutes and she started flat lining, the doctor told me to move that he was going to put her back on, I asked if she only had a few weeks, he said yes, only a few weeks, I said no.

I was holding my mother's hand she was squeezing my hand and staring at me, she couldn't talk. I looked at her and said no. Doctor said you're going to kill her, I said no I'm not she doesn't want the machine, he said move, she squeezed my hand and let go and closed her eyes and I laid over her body to keep him from putting the machine on her. She relaxed, and I whispered to her how much I loved her, and she was a good mother, and I'd be right behind her soon, and to be careful out there. Then she was gone.

I was in shock I couldn't sit down, I couldn't talk. It took me around two years to totally realize I did the right thing. They were going to do another exploratory surgery on her without our permission I didn't want her to have any more pain.

When my mother passed it was different than I thought it would be. I miss her, but my heart didn't hurt like with my daddy. My mother hardly ever bragged on me she always found stuff wrong with me. I know my mother loved me, but she just had a real hard time liking me because of her and daddy's marriage. She always said when I walked into the room: "Your just like your daddy", I was always in trouble. I watched my mother's spirit raise up out of the top of her head, it was gray & white I could see thru it. It seems like I have seen a lot of physical death in this life- time. Maybe I needed some lessons but now with that I've been enlightened to understand there is only physical death and then reincarnation to the next level each time. Karma is a word I didn't even know about I feel I chose these lessons and the participants also chose as I did. We are constantly Enlightened in all situations. That's my opinion. My grandmother made me promise her I wouldn't take any of her blood out of her body when she died at 94. And she wanted no new blood to keep her alive. You know it was so hard watching her starve/die, but I loved her so much I kept my promise. It took two weeks for her body to give in. How did she know she would need blood? All her blood dried up totally, so did her brothers, she knew that was going to happened that's why she told me she would haunt me if I gave her blood or put her in the ground without her own blood. She meant it Too!! She always said Jesus and God gave her all the things she ever needed. She has helped so many people on this earth.

Ida Verdie Johns was a true servant of our Divine Creator. I have always been close to Our Divine, when I was a child I was always asking for forgiveness, after I grew up, married, unmarried, now all the time I communicate all the time with Our Divine Creator.

I went to two different psychiatrist and included my children, both say I'm normal, that I'm a survivor, and have done a wonderful job in assisting my children, achieving a good profession, and that most people would consider my spiritual life a little **out of the box**, from both their opinions I've done quite well. I'm a normal mature gifted woman. Both of my children have seen the facts and know I'm fine. And respect my directions.

Within around two months after Mother left I was told to stop and look at this small place for rent. I had no idea what was going on. I looked at a place to rent for opening a business for people to come and learn about Metaphysical Spiritually & Enlightenment and to sell quartz crystal and other stones and crosses.

Without any consideration I looked at the space, it was small, very small but there was a bathroom without a shower. Room had an approximate 6-inch window across the top of one side and one door on the front. The rent was $300.00 dollars a month plus the lights. The words just came flowing out of my mouth I'll take it. I didn't know where I would get the money each month. I just knew I had to do it. I had a lot of crystals at home and older rosaries, crosses and books. So, I opened, it was two blocks from where I worked.

Several so-called Christians tried to make the City close my shop. God protected me

I was open every night after work and every weekend. I made some signs for my car doors, some cards

...yers. Within a month I had a lot of visitors, people would be there waiting for me to come the... ...her / Mother God and Jesus sent people to their little place in this small town. Of course, person... ...ted to put their stuff in the shop to sell so I did. At that time, I could see faces, places in crystals... ...t of people kept coming. I didn't want to, but I needed help paying the rent I started asking fo... ...ations for the crystal readings/visions. People in this small town were searching for this type o... ...ritual place to visit. People would come by and take their time looking and seeking informatio... ...n me, I have always told everyone it's not me, I'm a vessel Spirit speaks thru me. I read crystals, sav... ...es, places, being a vessel is humbling, as soon as I told / tell others thru spirit I forget what I say,... ...derstand that the message is for them not me.

...eally started buying crystals just right for each person's needs after talking to them expressing the... ...rsonal situations. I didn't make a lot of monies, but I was helping others and that was the who... ...son for having Realms Beyond. My daughter was very sick at this time, she had to have surgery o... ...e lymph glands it was horrible for her. I told her about the shop an asked her to name it she said rig... ...fore her surgery name it Realms Beyond, so I did. After a few months I started getting visits fro... ...rsons out of other towns, and other states. They were sent to share with me by spirit. During th... ...ne, I shared with so many beautiful beings of Love and Light.

...uring this time, I started getting validations from different persons telling me that the informatio... ...had channeled from spirit was starting to manifest with accuracy. That made me feel better becau... ...lways forgot everything channeled. That made me know I was right for trusting spirit. And tha... ...as doing what I was supposed to do. Friends, relatives, and others that knew me were very critical...

...ne time a woman stood outside my front door at the shop, she tried to step into the shop, she stopp... ...d said, why can't I come in, I told her you're not supposed to, that Realms Beyond is for people seeki... ...od's and Jesus's Love, and your beliefs don't agree with that. She said your right. It's not who or wh... ...am, I said goodbye and closed the door.

...ne day at work one if the women there asked if I would touch a friend's ring that had just died... ...ife had heard of me and wanted to see if I could reach him. During that day I wore the ring seve... ...mes and started picking up on him. I made a long list of the things I felt. The list was around... ...stimated around 10-15 different statements he had not been buried he was going to have a cremat... ...n a day or two. The wife called me before the laying of the cremation ashes into the Lake and aske... ...would come to the ceremony and after wards go to her house for a channeling of her husband. So,... ...riend at the office asked me also I said yes. I went to the ceremony and my friend and the wife were... ...ne boat a huge gator followed them way out into the lake and right behind them up to the shore. T... ...were so frightened the ashes were on them more than in the water. Weird!!!!!

...went to the home of the deceased it was dark. We, the three of us sat at the kitchen. Table.

...Here we go:

...prayed to God and asked for the deceased to come to us. All the dogs outside (three) of them sta... ...howling real loud then I started suffocating I could not breathe, it was like someone was choking...

His wife started telling him to stop don't hurt her she came to help me,

Finally, I could breathe he was still there inside but wasn't hurting me. It was like I could feel all his emotions; I started sitting different, I was sort of bending forward and propped my left elbow on my left leg then I was pointing to the howling dogs. The lady I worked with kept saying look at the way she's sitting, and how she's pointing her right hand towards the dog's. The wife said she is sitting like him, and he loves his dogs so.

I started getting real tired so we all asked him to leave my body, he did then I felt worn out. The wife told me then that he suffocated when he died. That was my first channeling I protect myself more now. The spirit man was very forceful.

At my job I really had to watch what I said, when I went to lunch my supervisor would follow me to me

shop, and then drive on by so I could see her. I kept my dog a beautiful Labrador white there during the day his name is: Sir Lance Sir Lot. Call him: Lance.

I was praying all during the day for protection from the evil around me. I didn't like being there. My place of employment (2001-2003 time) of over 20 years started making rules to get the old- timers to leave, or being written up for petty reasons, all employees were monitored all the time. I was followed on my lunch hour and timed to see if I would be late. I never was.

The historical section of town where I lived had a lot of beautiful old home houses. I was constantly guided to some of the dwellings to assist fragile spirits to leave the premises, lots of times stronger spirits would stop weaker spirits from leaving and keep them from going up to our Father / Mother God and Jesus. A lot of the reason was the way we are programmed from birth what is right and what is custom.

One night I was told to get up and go to a town just out of St. Augustine, I saw the home, and knew directions how to get there. Just knew. There was a spirit woman in the home she had been trying to communicate with the new owners. They were scared and putting the place up for sale. So, I drove up to the home, there was a real estate car in the driveway. I waited and a man that lived there came up to my car, I got out and said.,

I have something to tell you, you're going to think I'm crazy, I drove a long way to let you know the spirit woman in your home doesn't want you to move. He said just a minute, I'll get my wife, I thought boy I've done it now!! She came running out a very big tough looking woman, and said tell us, we don't want to move, but we are scared, and started telling me about all the movement and sightings in the home. They were so happy, it was their dream home, the spirit asked if she could stay and they were happy for her presence, I left and never saw them again.

A priest from our area visited me one day, he shared a lot with myself and several other people in the shop, I was told by a person that attended one of his sermons he brought up the little lady with the crystal shop, saying It was not evil that he felt the presence of God in that shop from everyone there. And rumors are wrong. judgmental and evil.

If you talked to others, employees talked they added things or situations to hurt others, and I was in a place to feel, read the ungodly persons emotions and/or purposes towards others. I fought with myself seeing the pure evil administered to others. I was talking to a man at my desk and asked him was he and his wife having a baby. He asked how you knew that. I replied just felt it. He told several other employees; another man came to me another day asked if his wife was pregnant I said yes. He said your right; how do you know I stated: Just felt it. They both told my supervisor and then she kept trying to find anything she could to fire me. So, I really had to learn to keep my job separate and not be so fragile in the public. The boss got to waiting at the door making sure no one was late even a minute. The point here is once you concede: there will be evil, as there is now. negative energy in many forms. But you are a spiritual entity in a physical body. You have all the power invested in you from our Father / Mother God and Jesus to protect yourself.

But, you are never alone your spiritual guardians, other spiritual beings, the Universal Entities of Love & Light are present just ask for help.

I was invited to see a woman at her house, that she felt a presence in her home, I went there and felt a young man in his early twenty that was in spirit. He didn't want to leave the building. He had taken his life there, and it was safe to him. Later I checked out the home at the library and there had been a death in the home.

Before, I left her home that night we were at a big table her and I and suddenly something hit my left leg knocking me backwards and the chair I was sitting in up against the wall breaking it to several pieces. I knew who it was and rebuked it in Jesus name, the woman saw everything and was speechless. My leg sometimes still aches.

At night It feels like someone pushes my shoulder to wake me up to get my attention. I can tell it's a good spirit, then usually I get directions to call someone, or go somewhere. Or feel something touching my face gently, or my hair.

You are so many in one!!!

We are all programmed to be what is expected by man. Awaken to your True Self!!

September 11, 2001:

On that day being a psychic/medium was very hard.

There were several people in the meeting room with the boss right across from me, the first tower had just been hit the news-caster kept saying looks like it will fall then the second one was hit I could feel the terrible energy from the television I kept feeling both towers will fall, saying nothing. Then the first one started falling my supervisor spoke up and said the second will not the broadcaster kept saying it's okay. It just came out from nowhere I said both are falling. Then the second one started falling, the he looked at me like he wanted to hit m

Some of the staff had a devotional time in the huge meeting room every week. The boss stopped us. He didn't like us meeting in the building doing bible quotes.

I started going to Psychic Fairs one day I had the honor of at least 13 individual personal readings that day. When you do readings unless you protect yourself from others energy, and attachments you may take several days to release those energies and attachments. Some people don't realize it but, they pull your energy away from you and you do have to clear yourself and rejuvenated your own energy. Pictures included showing auras, guides, these pictures are a true way to see firsthand your attachments, and many other important things.

I don't like doing readings in a group, people hear your own messages that don't apply to them. A lot of readers have very big egos!! The reason for sharing is to enlighten others, not put on a show!!

A woman who put some of her crystals and other things in the shop was going to Arkansas to dig in caves, mines, and asked me to go. I took two weeks' vacation and we left.

She was a different type of person and was very outspoken about everything. She had invited me to come over to her land to feel the energy there, so I did. I went on the property and could feel something was different we went into the southern part of her residence and I could really tell something was different I walked into this large room and immediately it was like I wasn't there physically.

It was like I was real cool and no gravity around me, I felt real light, energy wind surrounding me, she came and kept calling me and I looked at her as if she just walked into the big room, she said I had been there for quite some time. I felt like I had be on a road trip and just got back. *It* was a vortex.

She asked me to come back over to see if I could approach any deceased persons that come up to their residence all the time, she didn't want them there and had put up different types of crystals lots of stuff to keep them away, I said yes.

Here We Go:

I arrived there one afternoon no-one was there. I opened the gate and walked down the path/road to just before the front of the residence. I was told by spirit to take certain crystals with me. There was a fence all the way down their property line and they owned a lot of land. The lands attached were pastures lands too, hills and hills as far as I could see. I asked permission to pray. I remember feeling four different presence beings behind, the I asked where I put the crystals, spirit said: Put two on the ground and hold one in each hand. I looked up at said all those that want to move on show yourselves and come.

Then I saw hundreds of people: men, women, babies, all races, grieving, wanting help. Their eyes and faces were tired and worn out, then all the hills started filling up I asked anyone who was ready to leave and go to God to come within a hundred miles in a circle, they kept coming. There was a family group that would not go up with the rest of the people, they were real hard speaking but honest good people and their mother, brothers said they must protect the land. I said just wait till the others leave this man tried to scare me but the beings behind me kept him at bay. People just kept coming then thought they were people but they we spirit. Then I started praying saying things I don't remember bu do remember saying continually it's time to raise to your God. As I was praying with my eyes close remember that. The wind started blowing real hard all directions balancing myself I said rise up t God the wind was strong with my eyes open I saw the sky was mixing with pink clouds and blue cloud and then they were all gone except for the one family the father, mother, sister, and two men came u n front walking away from the tree on my left and I prayed again and I saw them all go as clouds int he sky then the wind totally stopped. I walked back to my car and left.

So, we did leave for Arkansas she drove her vehicle I was to split the expenses.

During the day drive as we approached cemeteries it was like gravity was pulling me to Raise my hand and pray for the people waiting to be with God like they had been taught to do for centuries just wait. raised both hands I would pray in the Name of Jesus for angels to assist people rise to their destination hat God wanted them to be. There were so many cemeteries going out there.

Then it was in the middle of the day my body was pushed up facing the door window my hands wer raised I started praying to another large group of people in a huge cemetery as we drove by I could se some many groups accentuation into the clouded sky with entities looking like angel beings. We wer by so fast the driver saw the whole thing of how my body was pushed. She didn't see the spirits.

One time I left some of the shops crystals at a business per their request. After about two month's I fe he need to pick the crystals up. So, I went on my lunch hour, drove there, left with the crystal towers aid them on my passenger side car seat, I was almost back to the office, and the largest crystal ser hought patterns saying: It's about time you picked us Up! Boy was I startled!!

Well we got to Little Rock, Arkansas and visited two crystal shops, I bought a lot. She bought some We went back to the motel and unloaded our stones

Here We Go: I must use insulin pen shots. I put my pens in the refrigerator and got ready for bed. The he woman said: You or your crystal can't ride back with me and I want you out of this room. She wa ooking like a totally different person, she said if you don't do as I say I will kill you.

very softly said why? She said you're seeing the real me now. (She was right she looked totally differen nd sounded different) I knew who she was.

said I will leave in the morning and I needed her to take me to the bus station, she said you'll have t pay me for gas and for this pick I thought you would need. I told her I would give her the gas but no pay for the pick that she'd bought that. She said okay.

My car was parked at her house. I laid there all night not knowing if I would be dead the next mornin or not she was over six feet tall and a good-sized woman.

fell asleep sometimes that night and went to take my insulin all five pens had been broken. She wa till asleep, so I went to the drug store and they gave me one pen to get me home the pharmacist sai ere all broken. I then saw a Fed-Ex place to send all my stuff home and give her gas money to ge down the mountain. She drove me down to the Hotel I got my suit case and she drove off. Leaving me stranded and broke over 1,400 miles from home. A soon as she drove off I knew God would get me home safely. I finally got in touch with my daughter and she wired me enough money to get home on a bus. I waited at that motel the usher kept my luggage for me and call me a cab in time for the bus after dark. They looked out for me all day. Then I was on the bus I prayed for God to locate anyone as we were going down different roads within 100-mile radius and let me constantly pray for persons (spirits) to rise to God in Jesus name.

Then I had to get off the bus in Atlanta, Georgia I was scared to I asked if I could please stay on the bus, the driver said no. I got off and started walking into the terminal it was packed. A man jumped in front of me another man put his hand on me took my pocketbook from around my neck threw me over the man in front and *was being thrown around like a rag doll. All the people around just watched. I got up off the floor noticing a security office and knocked on the door and told them what happened, and they said: Are you bleeding anywhere or been stabbed I said no, they said you're lucky. I had nothing now. I called my son as soon as I heard his voice I was in shock and handed the phone to the officer. He was going to drive up and get me but, the officer said we will make sure every driver watches her till she gets to you. After that I was unable to do any more spiritual work for around two weeks I was careful about being outside. I was spiritually and physically attacked.

My daughter moved into a nice house with a pool in town, everyone started to notice the wet foot prints in the bathrooms, I noticed two spirits in the home. They never bothered anyone.

I went to the Virgin Islands with my son, Before we left I was told by spirit to find the totem poles there and pray over the graves. To also sit out on the balcony and pray with certain crystal when I was in the Bermuda Triangle.

When we got there the three totem poles were at the hill on top of the cemetery full of graves. I prayed at the totems, and over all the graves. Then on the way back a storm was very bad, and I set outside and prayed with the crystals. We all thought the ship was going to turn over, it was bad. Bermuda Triangle lived up to it' s history.

For years I've noticed spirit forms not all are the same. Most are energy sparks. Or a white vapor.

We perceive spirit the way can handle it emotionally, mentally, spiritually We are all individual entities. Each of us have our own unique qualities.

I don't look for things to do, or people to talk to people just show up, I don't even keep cards on me, only give them out when someone asks for one. I'm not on a time schedule, spontaneous all the time. I do see events that are going to happen, like earth quakes, landslides, etc. I feel so much compassion it hurts, I cry a lot when I see anyone hurting, especially children.

When spirit comes into my vessel I must release it, or I explode inside, words must be spoken, actions must be done. I concede to Father / Mother God and Jesus,

Thought patterns are manifested by us. Your first thought pattern is usually spirit, we being humans add to our thought patterns making us confused. Actions are stronger than words. If you do not do anything negative towards any living creature words or actions you will become humble and act with love for all beings.

Remember our actions follow us for eternity, send love and receive love, sometimes it's hard to do when we are mistreated. Words are action also. There is a balance of negative and positive energy.

It is what it is!!!!!

We are programmed a at the time of our birth, what's right, bad, proper, accepted, etc. When we become mature we must make our own decisions, our parents, friends, will not be held accountable for our actions we will.

When I do readings a lot of the spirits want to let their love ones know their okay. **Usually most spiritual conversations are like, now I understand. I'm happy.**

Lots of family members want to live in the past, most spiritual beings talk about the future and seeing their loved ones again. A lot of spiritual beings stay around the ones they left until the physical person can manage on their own. We can hold our loved ones back by holding on to long. It takes a lot of energy from a spirit to be seen by their loved ones.

One night I noticed two children were missing on the news broadcast. I wrote down their names, looked up on the computer the name of their home town police department. Then thought patterns started working and wrote down the formation on paper. I kept seeing one child, a boy, in an old rustic barn, on a dirt road with hay in it he had an army blanket and was hungry, and cold. The road came from the town they lived in. But, it was like in a different world, the people were different, no houses. The boy was freezing to death and didn't have long. So, I called the Police Department.

They were very nice, understood what I was talking about, they got the boy, but it was too late, he had begun freezing. It was the way to the Indian Reservation, the girl was found okay, I didn't get anything on her.

It's always seemed like I should be able to handle physical death. Sometimes it's hard.

I have woke up remembering being around several different people assisting them to concede leaving their physical bodies and going to their new destinations. Children, and adults. I can describe everything in their surroundings. When the girl disappeared Natalie. I told my daughter what happened, and described the exact spot, next morning that spot was on the news, she had been washed out to sea. Sometimes I receive messages not to go down certain roads, I do pay attention. If I don't feel comfortable, I don't do or say it. I felt she had an allergic reaction to chemical she had ingested.

I noticed a sign on the side of the road for several months I was pulled to this sign with this woman's picture on it. This woman had been killed in the past few years, the Sheriff's Department was asking for help. So, I stopped and put my hands on the picture, I started seeing things, then I felt the urge to put my bare feet on it, I picked up a lot of things. Bet people who saw me thought I was interesting as they drove by. I put both of my bottom feet on the picture at different times, then I went back to the car and wrote down everything I had noticed. I called the officer's phone number and he was responsive, I was glad he was. He said he would check on everything, I gave him information he said he didn't have. Around 4-5 months later he called me and asked how I knew all that stuff, I said I didn't God did. They found the other bullet hole, found out about the little girl, and the make and color of the car, and that the second man was dead, and the one was in jail. When this kind when your gifted sometimes people can really drain you, everyone needs to make their own choices and not depend on others to do so for themselves. When energy happens, it makes you real sleepy, or tired. It takes time to get your normal strength back. Reading are the same, even more energy used with spiritual visitors around. We are all spiritual beings and all of us can do special gifts. So long as you concede to letting Our Divine Father Be in Control you will.

2005 thru 2011 I worked a lot, stayed home, still prayed but, didn't socialize much, I didn't want to be around people that much, I put all my effort into helping special needs persons, did stuff for a lot of different people, I would always tell them about our Divine Father, I worked for a large company and made sure the special needs of the people were met, I got real close to around seventy individuals. I enjoyed it, I would read for people that came to me, or called me needing help. I didn't shut down just became a home body and was waiting for an interaction from Divine to go where I should be.

## 2011

October 26, 2011, I made the change with Divines assistance, was starting to want a different <u>life other</u> than staying home and working seven days a week So I retired again.

First retired in 2003, then 2011. I wanted to be free to do spiritual work all the time

My daughter had opened the crystal shop and she was doing good, so I did readings out of her shop and wherever people wanted me too. I was told by spirit to write down some of my experiences starting from my childhood. So, I've tried to finish this for around twenty years. I've felt nobody wants to know of my experiences I'm just Sandy a regular person. But when you are woken up at night told to write you do it. <u>Spirit has told</u> me <u>even if only one person is given hope and enlightenment it's worth it.</u>

I am humble I thank Father / Mother God, Jesus and all The Holies for allowing me to be a part of the

Universal Enlightened. Trust your trust.

## 2012 Here we go again.

I prayed for Father/Mother God to send me a companion in my daily life someone of Divine choice.

Which I did. I prayed so many times asking for guidance of this person. He was the same as me. Out of the box!! We worked with crystals, prayed together and worked together. SEEMED I HAD MADE THE RIGHT CHOICE OF A GOOD COMPANION.

We started to be together all the time he fell in love with me and I fell in love with him he became my best friend. He was happy and so was I for six months. He put me first and truly cared for me. Then after six months he started to change his actions. We were so compatible even with our age difference of thirty-years. I moved back to Ocala with my daughter's assistance to be near her.

During this, I learned so much about many different things. People go thru things you'd never think could or would ever happen to you. I continued to do readings people who would seek me out like they were sent to me.

I feel I was given a chance to have had true love as I prayed for. That I helped him and myself with God's Accessions lessons and Karma on both his and mine sides have helped with Enlightenment Growth for both of us. I feel I was in love with love. I am thankful for the special friendship I shared, and I have eternity to remember.

<u>2018</u>

I will not concede to expose myself to negativity. It's hard sometimes because we are human still, but accession and enlightenment are Forever.

I reopened my shop again and I am meeting a lot of new people now. I continue sharing with the community in love & Light.

I Still do readings and learn something new every day. I meet a lot of beautiful people. The older

I get, the more things I notice during readings. I am content with my life and I am happy.

## Love & Light – Sandra Marie Holloway -

Crystals to receive vibrations during readings.

RUTILATED QUARTZ CRYSTAL

Amethyst Quartz

# Dessert Rose

Realmsbeyondocala@gmail.com
Sandrahollowaygrizzle@yahoo.com
(352) 682-8782

Book Review of:

Sandra Marie Holloway

Puts others first before herself, so proud of my friend Sandra Marie with no support or understanding as a child to witness and testify such amazing occurrences to share with those who listen. Thank you, Sandra Marie, For your courage.

Deseree J. Wessner, Certified Medical Technician